Saam Acupuncture Medi[...]
Thyroid and the 8's
The Accelerated Path

&

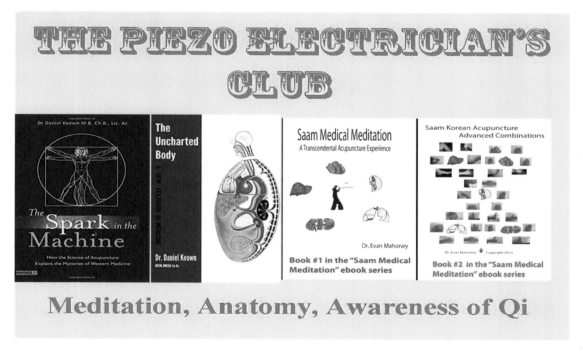

THE PIEZO ELECTRICIAN'S CLUB

Meditation, Anatomy, Awareness of Qi

Discourse on Dr. Daniel Keown's "The Spark in the Machine"

Dr. Evan Mahoney

Saam Acupuncture Meditation
Thyroid and the 8's, The Accelerated Path, The Piezo Electrician's Club
Discourse on Dr. Daniel Keown's "The Spark in the Machine"
Dr. Evan Mahoney, copyright 2018

Continuing from "Into the 8, The Eight Extraordinary Channels" and "Journal the Interpretation of Dreams V.1 E1." "Saam Medical Meditation" and other works available at Amazon.com.

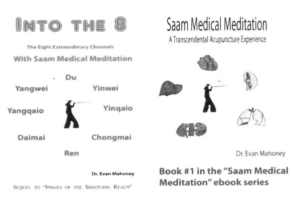

Thyroid and the 8's, The Accelerated Path
Saam Acupuncture Meditation

The Thyroid is a gland located below the Adam's Apple of the throat. Between it and the brain complex communication processes involving hormones and biological markers occur. The Pituitary gland responds (by releasing growth and other hormones) to levels of Thyroid Stimulating Hormone from the Thyroid.

The thyroid in the throat, are you aware?

Is yours riddled with phlegm?

Phlegm which mists shen and mind.
Leaving some stupid and dumbfounded.
Phlegm obstructs signals between the brain and heart, causing irregularities.

Do your hands and feet easily get cold? If yes, then don't bring cold into your body. No ice drinks, cold foods or exposures to cold. Don't walk barefoot on a cold tile floor or go under dressed.

****

I was close to drowning in a Swiss mountain lake. I ventured too far and felt a hypothermic panic encase my head. With trepidation I swam back to shore.

I tempted cold and lost, daring my back on a windy afternoon in the hills, coming down with a second attack of Sciatica the next day.

It wasn't until my acupuncture education that I learned about cold and what it had done to my life. I have made much better friends with cold hence forth. I dress warm, wear my socks, and drink warm ginger tea.

I have learned and overcome. I have become closely aware of myself through the unfolding meditation of Saam and Into the 8's.

Paradises of discovery continue to amaze, wonder, and delight.
Openings occur in unexpected, unimaginable manner.

Once more with my thyroid I am taken to a new level, upon the accelerated path.

11.27.18

Today in meditation I continue with the Spleen / SI and Chong and Dai mai channel meditations. These 8 extra's are the equivalent structures of wheat sheaves bundled at the waist. They form our spiritual and physical structure. Chong and Dai, blood and belt. In art, Vincent Van Gogh captured their archetype very well.

In cases of sexual depletion meditate upon the Spleen/ SI to restore essence, vis a vis Mingmen and duodenum (read further). The older you are, give longer periods of time to restore.

Yesterday I was kicked like a mule with an electronic spark at UB 20, 21 points (midpoint of spine just lateral to the 10th and 11th Thoracic vertebrae). This was the opening of a prior short or reversal of previous stroke. Based on its center middle location of my back I instantly knew it as a spleen or stomach manifestation.

My Spleen was deficient since early high school, when I coughed and hacked after running the mile. Phlegm, fluttered my heart irregularly, even unto today.

But I have control. I consider it a challenge, the calling moment of which to subside.
Through meditation I pick the channels. I grow, I learn in the experience, fine tuning my precision performance to find the inevitable blockage and break it down to rights.

My heart flutters were mere obstructions which I have far busted through, with meditation upon Qi and awareness of self.

The great science I study, I practice and heal from. In meditation I lay, in sweet peaceful repose and comfortable position. I consider myself a lucky man, or as my pastor would say "a blessed man".

I meditated on the thyroid with the Spleen/ SI and changed to Du and Ren.

The Ren channel!
A flutter like a constellation of stars! In movement Qi bubbled up the anterior part of my thyroid and throat.

The Accelerated Path
Or the other way around (decelerated) are part of our unfolding destiny.
It is interesting to pass from one into the other.

From Hypo to Hyper or into normal.
To change metabolism requires months, or years, not days. If one is able to accomplish it naturally at all?

The fortunate ones are well on their way to success.
Smart, sharp, strong, forceful, confident, quick.
Not a hiccup in their step or gut.

Good with people and therefore able to accomplish things.
Building on knowledge
The Earth is a grand reservoir of knowledge
Second only to Heaven.

You have the knowledge and etiquette to get along well in this world.
You have a sunny disposition.
People light up at your introduction.

You may not be trustworthy, but that don't matter one bit.
You are good company a Five Star type of guest.

The wheat sheave is a metaphor for health. An archetype from the eons stored in the spleen.

You sir or madam, are in fine form and expression.
Connected in body and mind, complete in the Spleen/ SI.

The throat is a tube of communication fibers packed tightly, conveying food, air, and information. Obstructions accord on their own, accounting for your near or far destiny, of going forth or holding back.

Through meditation I have moved forward in years well spent, seeking always the Accelerated Path.

****

11.29.18

My hands are like ice, against my wife's face
And to the neck of my neighbor, who questioned why I wore a scarf.
I am wearing gloves but haven't checked my inner Tom Sawyer.
Wearing socks with sandals, I am practically barefoot when I should be wearing shoes

My feet are as cold as ice. I can feel it without having to touch.

I am vulnerable to a stroke, a cold stroking out.
A whole body chill will occur, a spark in the brain, then panic. My breath will drop and I will pass out.

Knowing my vulnerability, I meditate on the Du and Ren rotating through all the Saam channels, mu's and whatnots.

I mirror the thyroid as my heart. All channels pass through each structure. In close proximity both are dense, mysterious. The blockage of my heart is the blockage of my Thyroid. By proxy I use the Thyroid to affect the heart.

The shaoyin source of my disease, my rheumy heart, right atrium, which once fibrillated and was squirmy, is threatening again with chest pains. I am aware of my poor habits.

A new stagnation was beginning which I have tackled in two or three days. Last night I was called to meditate upon the Liver based on two dreams which I've forgotten (an unheard of event!). I was the boss I think, in some firm manner. Turning over in bed I had a remnant pain in the chest.

It was 3:00 am. I meditated on the Liver then switched to Lung. Keeping attention to my chest with the 8's and Saam. I cycled through the Qiao's and the Wei's, running everything through the throat and thyroid as if sagitally. With hope and expectation of speeding my metabolism I have reached the deepest realm and source of my woe. Cold is in the upper chamber of my heart.

I still have my essence reserves. I do not feel exhausted of my Yin/ nor Yang. I do not think my arteries are blocked. In the warmth of my kitchen, as I type, my hands and feet warm up. I have recovered again.

My wife was so surprised at my cold hands this morning. Maybe she has a point, that I shouldn't do my morning breathing exercises or perambulations in the cold. In cold wind and socks I walked the path of my park.

Spleen / SI warmth of the earth gives comfort. The Wei's make all kinds of imaginable connections possible between the heart and thyroid, and mu's, etc. First using the Liver then Heart/ GB with Du Ren, Qi flowed the occipital, back of my throat, and posterior thyroid to my heart. Reliving and curing a thousand obstructions. At the deficiency stagnation area of my chest I moved Qi above and below, becoming fuller in form.

Thyroid is alive now, calling forth the Kidney / San Jaio which is the appropriate response to recover from cold wind stroke. This is a correct and true conclusion, a law of science. The Kidney warms. Wind is housed in the Shaoyang, there are diseases and strokes of cold and heat. Of Heart heat or Kidney cold. One in raving phlegmatic mania, the other stiff and silent.

This has been a "How to Recover" from cold wind, using meditation and common sense.

I still must pay attention to the pain in my chest. The possibility and concern of heart attack is there yet. Into the Kidney /San Jaio I now go, with the 8's too. A very nice meditation ensues.

I send Kidney healing power to restore the structures of my heart, then move to the Heart / Gall Bladder. Qi is dense in the Thyroid. Energetic proxies of every heart murmur I've ever had occur in benign form, in movement of Qi. The Thyroid Pineal system is communicating. I feel hormones release as if they were pixie dust of stars scratching my throat settling to the heart. I remember the Qaio's, of stem cells, form and structure. Reparations are being made.

For some time I am in the Heart/ Gall bladder, thyroid and heart. Then I move into the Pericardium/ Stomach passing from the direct source and urgency of the matter. The pericardium is protector of the heart and absorbs the less fatal blows. Stem cell reparations too are being sent here too vis a vis the Qiao's, Du and Ren.

My thyroid is full in Qi.

The Invisible Function - Heart

The heart dominates the realm of sleep. It is in sleep that we as babies (and adults) grow. The heart is the monarch and architect for the grand design of our being. It is in our sleep that blood vessels form, tissue grows, and channels reach ever outward and inward, all under the quiet direction of the heart. Sleep well and both growth and healing occur. The ruler who rules the least, rules the best. - Saam Medical Meditation

The Constellation - Heart, Thyroid, Pituitary

As the Kidneys (Shaoyin channel) has the adrenal glands, the Heart (Shaoyin channel) has the Thyroid and Pituitary Glands (my own theory, which is ok to be skeptical of), which hormonally interact vis a vis a feedback loop, first of measurement then of action.

All channels (communications) pass through the heart. The Thyroid mirrors (Acupuncture Mircrosystem Theory) as an energetic proxy, the heart (imo).

The Eight Extraordinary Channels

The Wei's connect. The Qaio's (ren / du) send the hormones, stem cells, or fold and continue to grow.

****

My dear mother has come down with an illness that includes significant pain. Both my parents are elderly and I worry they may be going where my sister went.

I pray for my mom and intervene for her to God.

"Oh dear, Lord," I fervently pray and meditate on the Heart / Gall Bladder and Du 20 (LN). I tap into the unconscious, adding GB B +. I am in the thyroid and the upper chambers of my head.

"There is nothing, there is nothing," an answer comes not.

I switch to the Lung / UB. (UB which runs anterior to Pituitary connects with the Lung in Harmonized combination).

The Lung - Realm of the Mortal Soul. The Ho Spirit knows it is dying.

"Poor, poor mortal soul," I cry thinking of my mom.

Salty tears run down my cheeks. I am in my forehead on the other side of death, while still living.

I have an indication of the Ho soul's travel. It will take the form of a frog.

A frog buried in mud, sitting in a remote swamp lake. My tears fall for me, to forget and wash me anew in new form and find myself once more content, calm. Some animals are calm unto the point of death.

My sadness is well and properly contained in the Lung / UB, Pituitary, Thyroid, Ren and DU (it will not linger nor cause me harm as before). It has already transformed!

Calm and comforted, with wet tears still on my cheek, I return back to the Heart and find a well spring of great joy. Joy and Trust for the world, of what will happen.

There will be sorrow followed by joy. Tears of salt wash memories and promise life. Some animals exhibit trust better than We.

But I can't accept that we become frogs.
Moments later I am in meditation again still on the Heart.
"Make her an Angel," I pray.

Angels! And the crown of my head opens. The old halo.

"Dear Lord, send Angels," and the Lord made an Angel of me.

I felt as if transported due North twelve miles to my mother's bedside, palpable surrounding, clearly defined. She is sleeping or resting, then has a moments passing shock at my visitation, Angels of hope are upon her.

In this way I will pray, to send Angels and become one myself.

The Ho Spirit goes to the frog but the immortal goes with Angels.

****

The Du Ren Cerebellum

I have always felt it heavenly, a cool autumn wind and an afternoon Indian Sun of a season shortened day. I used to have such days and afternoons in forests and brooks of Pennsylvania, sitting on rocks, with winter soon on the way. Purity is frozen. Cold matron saints have come to me in lessons and visions, of rebuke and gentle punishments and brief moments of encouragement.

What comes next after sending Angels?
Receiving Angels (I draw the A with wings and a halo).

I received Angels at the crown of my head. Angels poured fountains of knowledge upon my head. As like a waterfall they were over me. Kneeling and pouring forth from a cauldron, golden streams of light. They seemed to enjoy doing such a thing,

My Cerebellum became delineated.

Eureka! A Heavenly Reign. I already knew and anticipated this, moments before its occurrence.

This is an area of the Shaoyang Realm. Don't let the unconscious Bugaboo's keep you from the Heavenly Realm, they stick upon the screen, obscuring the vision.

Clear your intractable stress, usually from intractable relationships. These are winds of the Gall Bladder Shaoyang Realm. These are the insults taken and given. Insults difficult to forget, of family stress and disturbances, clear away with GB B+ (Saam Acupuncture: Advanced Combinations). Every step in the way of Qi is bliss, be pleasant and thankful.

Let nothing disturb the purity of your interaction with heaven.

Fall is the season of the Lung. It is fall now. 12.5.18

****

Something funny happened yesterday when I performed at the audition rounds for a big television show. It was at the convention center in Tampa with about three thousand participants. The audience was typical of what is seen on the show. I watched child struck as a man performed balloon tricks and figures. Carnival Girls in bikini's and tall feathers rehearsed their dance and took lots of pictures of themselves. A Jersey looking Goombah and female Elvis impersonator bobbed and weaved in similar fashion as a camera panned over them through several takes.

Young Ok noted that most of the people looked like Shaoyang Korean Constitutional Body types, with narrow faces and beautiful features.

She said of them and me, "The Shaoyang's need to be doing this."

To be in performance is a level three Liver need. Liver is the dominant energetic aspect of the Shaoyang body type.

I was on the outskirts of the crowd going through with my plan. Meditating a lot on the thyroid and then at 30 minutes before performance begin to practice. I was playing Jerry Garcia's "To Lay Me Down". As I stood among the crowd of my peers I looked about and noted that nobody upstaged me (good sign giving confidence).

Too shortly though I was called to the room. Our group was led to the sparse auditorium with a producer sitting behind an empty table. She seemed a fair and impartial judge and revealed little through body language.

As we waited for the other people before me to perform, my phone rang. It caused a slight panic with my wife and I. I took the phone and thought I turned the volume down. Soon I was called to perform.

I told the judge this was an old canal song, sung in the 1830's. A Muleskinner Song called "My Sweetie is a Mule in the Mine". I dedicated it to my wife.

I started poorly. I was playing and singing too slow. Uh Oh.

From an acting book I recently read I reminded myself to look at my fingers and imagine them as the fingers of a real true muleskinner (which I was). The pace picked up. The judge's head jumped when I sang "spit" which comes at the end of the second to last line of every verse.

I had to look at her as I finished with the words of the final verse "All day I sit, I chew and spit, all over my sweety's behind." Before I got to the line I realized how silly it was going to be to have to look at her and sing this.

"Dang it"… I was kicking at a fence post afterwards, exiting the convention center.

"Dang it, Dang it, Dang it," it didn't go well.

Later, I remembered as I performed, I had paused mid song to turn around and look at my wife. As I did so she was paying absolutely no attention to me. Sitting at about the eighth spot out of twelve people, she was bending away from me and reaching towards the ground with both her hands.

"That is odd," I thought as I turned back to finish the song.

Later in the car she was a bit angry with me. The phone had rung again. It turns out I hadn't lowered the volume.

Even though it didn't go well it was still entertaining. The audition holding room was my level three moment, though brief it was. I stood among performers and felt their attention upon me. None had risen to upstage me.

All day long I had been meditating upon my thyroid as I had planned. I was very calm and very observant of the rush of adrenaline and wave of nervousness that occasionally passed. My heart was in a jittery mode with the uptick in pressure, but I managed it very well.

My back was sore today from all the sitting and waiting of yesterday. I did intensive stretching with the inversion table, hanging, and psoas stretches off both the treatment table and trunk of my car.

The lower back pain also called attention to the Lung/ UB technique with the added Qiao's as the primary 8. My lower spine was targeted. That old L4-L5. The next day I stretched out the psoas very well and returned to a healthy pain free comfortable straight and upright posture. This is the indication of the Lung / UB, when hunched forward the Lung is supposed to straighten you back up. I did so with stretching and the Qaio's added.

I also imagined the kidneys and the adrenal gland function, as somewhat similar to that of the thyroid only dominating the lower jaio. With the Lung / UB I may have connected to the pineal gland in the brain, or the pituitary. The UB channel at the back of my head lit up, as did my lumbar spine and sacrum.

I imagined as if a fan belt was operating between the different glands. One between the adrenal and pineal (or pituitary) and one with the pituitary and thyroid, and one between the adrenal and the thyroid. All was running smoothly between one another.

With this I also added the Du Ren and also the Kidney/ San Jaio. These were targeted meditations of the lower jaio and lumbar spine. Maybe stem cells were sent to these places too?

Self Exorcism

Go straight to GB B+ (as part of the Heart/ GB Harmonized).

Beware of sin, reject haunting spirits, and evil synchronicities. Pray to heaven, the Angels, bind your love to Jehovah and his Son incarnate.

Expel the bad wind using GB B+. Bring the Good wind from above using the same.

Have good relationships. Send out Angels of love to your enemies. Receive Angels of love.

Expel bad wind and evil spirits using GB B+

****

Treatment for Grief

I was complimented by my patient who I last treated for grief.

"You are a great doctor," she said to me.

I used Saam Acupuncture Meditation technique, Lung/ UB.

Grief is a physical disease and it resides in the Lungs.

Grief comes like waves of Qi, Grief is a palpable sensation (of Qi).

I instructed her to meditate upon the Lung tonifying points on her right arm and leg.
I asked her to call her grief. When it comes, send it far out of her head to the meditation points on the hand and feet. Do this both during and after the treatment.

She is a Qi responsive patient. She feels Qi well.

In acupuncture and meditation grief rolls in waves.

In Saam Acupuncture Meditation, channel grief.

****

On the dock, towards the North Star I kneel and pray.

Oh Jehovah
Oh Monarch and Judges
Oh Heart / Gall bladder
Oh Love / Courage
Hallelujah

"I am healed," I think.

Moments later I hear Joel Osteen (I am not a fan of prosperity preaching) inside my house. Sermon titled "The Promise is Coming."

God has a plan for us, he foreknows everything about us, about every mistake and every misfortune. God has a promise in spite of our tough and hard circumstance.

"You may have been given a diagnosis saying, you will just have to live with it. Well God has another plan for you."

12.30.18

I am concerned about atherosclerosis. I probably have a mild case of inflammation in the blood vessels from too much extraneous heat. I eat a lot of cheese, chocolate, and fatty foods. I am about 5 pounds overweight and am 48.

These mild aches in my chest set off alarm bells which begin my immediate meditation intervention. The two acupuncture points I combine with the Saam are Spleen 10 and Lung 9. Spleen 10 is the invigorate blood point and Lung 9 is the influential point of vessels. (This is Coronary Artery Meditation: in The Knowledge Pursuant Self).

The purpose of my meditations is to invigorate blood and target it to my blood vessels. With each Saam Point prescription I feel Qi moving in my chest within the arteries and vessels of my heart and throat. I get typical Qi spasms and convulsions that I equate with growth and healing. My pulse is more full and forceful, less deep and sluggish.

So far so good.

Just wanted to impart this for those who might also have atherosclerosis concerns.

****

The Piezo Electrition

I am on my second reading of Dr. Daniel Keown "The Spark in the Machine" in preparation for my forthcoming order of "The Uncharted Body".

I think what Dr. Keown is teaching me is that fascia and collagen fibers enfold most every structure in the human body. The bones, fascial planes, organ surfaces, artery vein surfaces(?), and brain surfaces (?) are probably composed of collagen which has Piezoelectric properties. A bend in the fiber produces a spark like the bending of crystal when striking a lighter. A bend in the bones from weight bearing exercise produces a spark at places of most tension, signaling for the osteoblast development of bone tissue.

I believe Dr. Daniel Keown is setting up the question of whether humans can (and already do) regenerate themselves, though preposterous the idea. Is limb regeneration possible like a Salamander's? The short answer is "no" because our blood does not contain specialized DNA for regeneration as does a reptile.

What about the long answer? What about the Piezo Electrician? Aware of Qi and able to conduct it along the multitudinous folds of collagen fascia covering the organs and structures.

What about the Piezo Electrician who with intelligence can move and manipulate these energies? Can one skilled in such a manner regenerate? I believe it is so.

Atherosclerosis Meditation

Incorporate Lung 9 and Spleen 10 with your regular Saam channel point prescriptions. Lung 9 is the influential point of vessels, Spleen 10 invigorates blood.

When doing this with Saam Medical Meditation Heart / Gall Bladder harmonized combination you are targeting the arteries and vessels of the Heart and Gall Bladder. My chest pains and areas of stagnation have dispersed alleviating my concerns. My blood pressure yesterday and today was 122/ 73, encouraging.

The Lung / UB also targets the chest area. Lung 9 is already the tonifying point of the Lung Jungguk.

In using the Spleen / Small Intestine harmonized combination the Spleen channel is further invigorated with Spleen 10. After the stagnation was dispersed in the chest it moved to the carotid arteries on the neck. Using this meditation I was able to target these and other vessels under my jaw (spleen area) creating openings and dispersions.

It is interesting whenever I encounter an area of stagnation and I incorporate Lung 9, Spleen 10 I feel the Qi worm at the artery at Lung 9 and 8 on both sides. The Qi worm slithers, spasms, and convulses. This is a microcosm of what is also happening in my arteries. Venture into new areas of stagnation (which are plentiful in a densely compacted manner) and you can get the Qi worm slithering and dredging its way through blockage.

The Pericardium/ Stomach also directly targets the chest and stomach and Ren line (with influential points of PC and Stomach). I will also incorporate the Ren / Du channel with the relevant Saam Channel point prescriptions (as well as other eight extra meridians).

The Kidney/ San Jaio and Lung 9, Spleen 10 is interesting. You can target the chest areas along the upper Kidney channel points. Lung 8 is tonifying point #2 of the Kidney Jungguk it is only 1 cun adjacent to Lung 9. Maybe this closeness to the influential point of vessels is related to the essential hypertension diagnosis, which is high blood pressure attributed to Kidney pathology, usually intervened with diuretic medications.

With all the Saam channels you can get a soothing effect on the arteries with the use of Lung 9, Spleen 10.

It is interesting to incorporate Dr. Daniel Keown's explanation of control centers and cell fractal growth and division with Saam Medical Meditation. With meditation upon Qi you can physically feel these processes. You can direct and target these processes to anywhere in your body. In "The Spark in the Machine" he states that repeated carcinogen exposure influences cell division and growth, turning the cell away from its own body signals and how the body wants the cell to grow. I propose with Qi meditation one can influence proper cell growth and repair.

****

Dr. Keown relates remarkable information on the heart. Among them are anecdotes on heart transplant patients and how they interact with the donor's family and loved ones (whom they have never met before) as well as the following passage from page 133 "The Spark in the Machine".

"The heart's electrical system is neurological in nature. The conducting system of the heart is effectively the same as the brain, relying on the same nerve energy to create its effect…. If one person spends a lot of time with another then the constant interplay of their electromagnetic heart activity will subtly affect each other's hearts…. Electromagnetic forces affect other electromagnetic devices… When your loved one feels something sad or exciting, that change in heart energy will travel as electromagnetic impulses as fast as light…Even before these hit you, your heart will move because if your hearts are in quantum entanglement then this occurs instantaneously!"

From the same passage, "In science, the beautiful phrase is quantum entanglement: poets call it love."

This begets an assumption of synchronicity between loving people, but what of the difficult family situations? Of the intractable stressors of difficult family relationships and situations?

In "Structure's of Knowledge" it is these intractable stressors that affect persons at the unconscious. For this we use the harmonized combination of Heart/ Gall Bladder with Gall Bladder B+ points. It is the Gall Bladder B+ points and the GB's energetic aspect of "outward moving wind" that can help expel these unconscious bugaboos. Would these unconscious bugaboos not be some kind of discordant electromagnetic static between difficult partners or family situations affecting the heart's optimal performance? Expel these static stressors with the GB B + points as an outlet.

****

Touched by an evil pathogen.

In my dream a few nights ago 3.15.19 I was homeless and sleeping on the floor in a flophouse. A girl was sleeping on the couch above me. I reached out and touched her hand. She squeezed my hand. It was a warm gesture full of heart and love.

Immediately after a scary voice from behind me said "What about me?" and a deep chill seized me at the back of my neck (UB guardian). Without looking at who is talking I whisper a shivering "who are you?" over my shoulder and realize I am frozen in fear.

I wake up. There is a deep chill at my neck. My blanket is thrown off my shoulders and a cold wind draft is upon me. I am asleep on the floor as I often do and wonder about dust from the carpet.

Most of my dreams for weeks preceding this had to do with a wandering homelessness and dissatisfaction with my homeland (a lung deficiency). So it was with the dream of being homeless in a flophouse, although the moment I squeezed the girls hand was a moment of heart love. Immediately after or during this hand squeeze is when I was touched by the evil spirit. I fear the evil pathogen has gone directly to my heart.

The next day I have a sore scratched throat and lose my voice. I also have dull spasms and aches to my right Kidney area and a momentary instance of heart pain. This pathogen has indeed entered me at a deep level. I am afraid for potential inflammation of the heart and blood vessels.

Along with an inflammatory wind I presume to have a deficiency of Kidney Yang and Mingmen fire which makes me prone to cold attack. With the intent to warm and tonify my Jing essence, I recall Dr. Keown's theory of Mingmen being in the duodenum and am reminded again of how the earliest Sages from ancient China emphasize that Mingmen is contained in the right kidney, the right side.

This inspires me to do a Spleen/ Small Intestine harmonized combination visualized to the duodenum and I get strong responses along my spine, right side from the Spleen back shu points down the spine to DU 4 (Mingmen) and Small Intestine. Perhaps these points along the spine represent the twelve inches of the duodenum? Rooted at Mingmen, un-separated along the way.

During my meditation I double up on combinations like using the Spleen and Lung, Taiyin organs with their harmonized Taiyang at the same time. Or I combine Heart and Kidney Shaoyin, connecting my heart left side with Kidney right side. I connect through a kink I feel as if on the aorta between my right Kidney and Heart. I also connect my heart with the duodenum (Small Intestine) through the Ligament of Trietz. I am energetically super busy at the deepest points.

I am loading up and flipping through all these channels and connecting points, feeling the convergence of Qi in all the proper deep locations along the spine, aorta, right kidney, heart, lung, and spleen.

I feel as if I am tapping into my Kidney Jing Essence and using vast storehouses that were frozen out. Mingmen fire, alight and save me! My recent writing retirement signified a decline, a lack of purpose, of death. Neural crest cells are sent to heal my areas of inflammation, obstruction, or disease and perhaps give me life again.

The night of the evil pathogen I did not sleep well. The next night I slept better and then last night I had very pleasant dreams relating to my homeland. In last night's dream I revisited scenes and places I had grown up in. They were pleasant, comforting, and well built out with plentiful material possessions. Based on the pleasantness of my dreams I feel the pathogen has passed. I have opened up new deep areas through what is probably a release of neural crest or stem cells.

I am back in Zygote Meditation (magazine article 2015) and have tapped into my yolk and maximized my digestive efficiency which nourishes Jing Essence.

My previous month's dreams of homelessness left a vulnerability in the lungs, chest, and heart.

"Your face looks red," my wife said to me today. Later I looked in the mirror and couldn't believe how bright cherry red my entire face was. Lots of blood is moving. I am growing. My blood pressure is low.

****

The Piezo Electrician's Club - For Meditators and Anatomists and those who are in the know on the experience Qi.

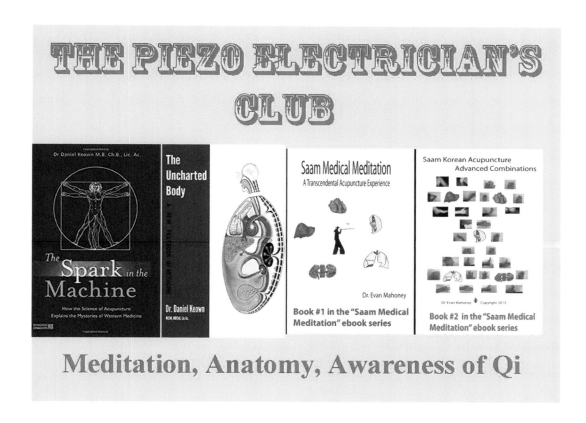

THE PIEZO ELECTRICIAN'S CLUB

Meditation, Anatomy, Awareness of Qi

This morning I was sitting on the dock. In meditation on the Pericardium / Stomach I was transported back to the waters of Still Pond on the Chesapeake Bay, a place where our family frequently anchored.

This morning's chop and the bay colored water reminded me of those moments when I was a young boy. I have a life's worth of knowledge, of waters where I swam and played.

****

Last night's dream had me pulling a hunk of phlegm from my throat like it was a thick piece of cheese. Perhaps due to the fish fry we attended last night. I also finished reading "Spark" with the ending chapter on the Gall Bladder and how it regulates lymph and tendons.

Waking, I meditate on the Heart/ Gall Bladder with Ren channel added to access the lymph that was the real indication of my dream. I visualize the Gall Bladder with the Cistern of Chyli and get the targeted Qi response and movement within these areas. Lymph is moving and circulating even at Stomach 12 "Dr. Daniel Keown's Que Pen" node.

I am grateful for Dr. Daniel Keown's "Spark in the Machine". I am surprised at how much I missed upon my first reading of the book. Dr. Keown has greatly aided in my visualization and targeting of the internal organs and structures, for this I think he saved a part of my life.

His books are probably the finest most detailed account of eastern and western anatomy combined. They are a ground breaking work. Through references in journals, broadcasts, and publications (not so unusual as mine) I hope he receives recognition.

He has breathed new life in the study of anatomy; he has introduced "Spirit".

Now on to "The Uncharted Body".

****

The Piezo Electrician II - Expanded usage of the Lou Connecting Points

The Archangel Gabriel granted me permission to surmise. Dr. Daniel Keown might be a blessed communicator, inspired by Angels who impart the highest levels of knowledge. Such is the tone of joy, enthusiasm, and surety of subject in his books.

I think Dr. Keown is akin to a neural crest cell, shaping in plaster our highest levels of understanding of Anatomy, Embryology melded into the structures of Qi and Jing Lou pathways.

There is great insight to be found for those in the experience of meditation and awareness of Qi. There is much that will help one grow and live longer than otherwise might be. How can one not be blessed who has gained great knowledge and self experience of such things?

I was touched at the heart and became familiar with electronic pathology. Across a dozen years I had multitudes of concerning episodes, brought under control by meditation. I felt Qi before I knew what it was.   I have never since stopped knowing about it.   To come into understanding of Acupuncture and Oriental Medicine and its history satisfies my level three human needs for knowledge. It leaves me in awe as I feel it must leave Dr. Keown as well.

Dr. Keown's translations of Chinese medical ideograms and his interpretations of the acupuncture points are satisfying. His illustrations of the pressure/ electrical channels and Qi dynamics are imaginative. His drawings (as of the body on the cover) are beautiful and informing, signifying space which are part of the essential discovery of Qi physiology.

I am willing to declare Dr. Keown's work; genius and artistry.   I suspect he might be a Renaissance Man.

I am grateful for his passion on behalf of acupuncture. I am grateful for his enthusiasm as a western medical doctor.   There is no doubt on the existence of Qi. There is no doubt on the remarkable similarities of ancient Chinese medical ideograms with discoveries of modern medicine, studied with modern technology.

****

The Piezo Electrician will do well to have a belief in Angels, you will be closely touched by them.

The Piezo Electrician will understand the highest levels of knowledge.

****

"The Uncharted Body" has inspired me to amend my position on the use of the Lou connecting points, which I have done formerly with the opposite clock channel location (Advanced Combinations).

Pleasingly I feel liberated and now am inclined to think about using Lou connecting points of the harmonious channel combination prescriptions.

If I am using Liver /LI, I may choose the Lou connecting point of the Liver or LI and then connect it further to the Gall Bladder or Lung Lou connecting points.

This provides satisfying for the Lung / Urinary Bladder harmonized combination because now we get the Kidney involved with its Lou connection to the Bladder. Lung is already the mother of Kidney. The Du / Ren's too. All help to preserve our precious Kidney's.

I feel comfortable with the Heart/ Gall Bladder and Pericardium / Stomach harmonized combinations. They are already opposite clock partners for the Lou connecting point. I now add the Small Intestine to the Heart and think about the Mingmen connection and valvular connection through what I have learned with Dr. Keown.

I appreciate the differentiation of the Jing Well points when doing the Pericardium or Heart Saam Acupuncture/ Meditation point prescriptions. For years I have corrected my heart electrical signals with Ht/ Gb and focus on Heart 9 and Liver 9. The Pericardium (use of Jingwell point Pc 9) for blood to the heart and arteries which I have recently documented.

With these meditations I have connected to my thyroid, tongue, throat, underside of jaw and deep places of the back brain.

I rejoice at the many ways to make connections through meditation on Qi, achieved with new found knowledge.

****

Yesterday I walked and remembered a sin.
"Lord, forgive me of my sins." I meditated upon the channels and prayed to Jesus.

This morning's church sermon taught by Cindy Grasse I learn the meaning of "Justification."

"The Lord will Justify you," through the sacrifice of Jesus, who took upon himself your sin. No matter how great and ugly is too much for him.

Justification - means "Just as if, it never happened".

Today the Lord has Justified me.

The sin I remembered, I remember not.
Just as if, it never happened.
Just as if, it never happened.
How simple and wonderful?

I am on the Liver / LI using the harmonized Lou's. Now that I am justified how goes it with my level three need? Was it sin that has thus hindered me? Yes, it was. Thus far I have been corruptible. The Lord will not allow me to proceed.

With the Liver /LI Jungguk I am on Liver 5 and Gall Bladder 38 left side, connecting the Lou's of the Liver / GB.

Smoothly it goes, smoothly.

****

On Spiritual Matters - Christianity, Buddhism, and Daoism

According to Alfred Adler's inferiority complex theory; those born with a weak organ or element will work hard to overcome that deficit and thus strongly develop skills and characteristics associated with that deficient organ or element. This is akin to somebody born with weak lungs eventually becoming a singer.

So it is with my heart health issues that I have been drawn to the spiritual. My shen is probably strong and eccentric. Every day I am frequently in prayer as I am frequently in meditation. I was raised a Christian and Catholic and pray to God Jehovah, Jesus, the Archangel's Gabriel, Michael, and Raphael. I read through the entire Bible each year to deepen my understanding with the Word and Nature of God. I encourage others to do the same.

*

Following are excerpts from a book I found in a local Good Will store. The book is called "Chinese Civilization; A Sourcebook", edited by Patricia Buckley Ebrey, second edition copyright 1983, published by Free Press.

The book is comprised of portions of ancient texts through the historical periods of China translated by different interpreters.

Chapter 34 (p. 146) titled "Precepts of the Perfect Truth Daoist Sect" is a translation of a 13th Century Daoist Sect called "The Perfect Truth" founded by eccentric ascetic Wang Zhe (b. 1180). It characterizes the learning of Sages and Monks of the Perfect Truth. Following are some excerpted chapters, translated by Whalen Lai and Lily Hwa.

"On the Cloistered Life"

"All those who choose to leave their families and homes should join a Daoist Monastery, for it is a place where the body may find rest. Where the body rests, the mind also will gradually find peace; the spirit and the vital energy will be harmonized, and entry into the Way (Dao) will be attained.

In all action there should be no overexertion, the vital energy is damaged. On the other hand, when there is inaction, the blood and vital energy will become sluggish. Thus a mean should be sought between activity and passivity, for only is this way can one cherish what is permanent and be at ease with one's lot. This is the way to the correct cloistered life."

"On Cloud - Like Wandering"

"There are two kinds of wandering. One involves observing the wonders of mountains and waters, lingering over the colors of flowers and trees; admiring the splendor of cities and the architecture of temples; or simply enjoying a visit with relatives and friends. However, in this type of wandering the mind is constantly possessed by things, so this is merely an empty, outward wandering. In fact one can travel the world over and see the myriad sights, walk millions of miles and exhaust one's body, only in the end to confuse one's mind and weaken one's vital energy without having gained a thing.

In contrast, the other type of wandering, cloudlike wandering, is like a pilgrimage into one's own nature and destiny in search of their darkest, innermost mysteries. To do this one may have to climb fearsome mountain height to seek instruction from some knowledgeable teacher or cross tumultuous rivers to inquire tirelessly after the Way. Yet, if one can find that solitary word which can trigger enlightenment, one will have awakened in oneself perfect illumination; then the great matters of life and death will become magnificent, and one will become a master of the Perfect Truth. This is true cloud-like wandering. "

"On Book Learning"

"... Thus one should diligently cultivate the inner self, never letting one's mind run wild, lest one lose his nature and destiny. If one cannot fully comprehend the true meanings of books, and only tries to read more and more, one will end merely jabbering away before others, seeking to show off one's meager talent. "

"On the Art of Medicine"

"Herbs are the treasures of the hills and the waters, the essence of the grass and the trees. Among the various herbs there are those which are warm and those which are cold; properly used, they can help in supplying elements to or eliminating them from the body. There are active and less active medicines, those that work externally and internally. Therefore people who know thoroughly the power of herbs can save lives, while those who do not will only do further harm to the body. Therefore the man of the Way must be expert in this art. But if he cannot be, he should not pursue it further because it will be of no use in the attainment of the Way and will even be detrimental to his accumulation of merits."

"On Sitting in Meditation"

"Sitting in meditation which consists only of the act of closing the eyes and seating oneself in an upright position is only a pretense. The true way of sitting in meditation is to have the mind as immovable as Mount Tai all the hours of the day, whether walking, resting, sitting, or reclining. The four doors of the eyes, ears, mouth and nose should be so pacified that no external sight can be let in to intrude upon the inner self. If ever and impure or wandering thought arises, it will no longer be true quiet sitting. For the person who is an accomplished meditator, even though his body may still reside within this dusty world, his name will already be registered in the ranks of the immortals or free spirits and there will be no need for him to travel to far - off places to seek them out; within his body the nature of the sage and the virtuous man will already be present. Through years of practice, a person by his own efforts can liberate his spirit from the shell of his body and send it soaring to the heights. A single session of meditation, when completed, will allow a person to rove through all the corners of the universe."

"On the Union of Nature and Destiny"

"Nature is spirit. Destiny is material energy. When nature is supported by destiny it is like a bird buoyed up and carried along by the wind - flying freely with little effort. Whatever one wills to be, one can be. This is the meaning in the line from the *Classic of the Shadowy Talismans:* "The Bird is controlled by the air." The Perfect Truth Daoist must treasure this line and not reveal its message causally to the uninitiated. The gods themselves will chide the person who disobeys this instruction. The search for the hidden meaning of nature and mind is the basic motif of the art of self cultivation. This must be remembered at all times."

"On the Path of the Sage"

"In order to enter the path of the sage, one must accumulate patiently, over the course of many years, merit -actions and true practices. Men of high understanding, men of virtue, and men who have attained insight may all become sages. In attaining sage hood, the body of the person may still be in one room, but his nature will already be encompassing the world. The various sages in various Heavens will protect him, and the free spirits and immortals in the highest realm of the nonultimate will be around him. His name will be registered in the Hall of Immortals, and will be ranked among the free spirits. Although his bodily form is in the world of dust, his mind will have transcended all corporal things."

The end of passage.

Thus it is how I feel when I pray to Jehovah, Jesus, the Angels, and Saints and ask protection and guidance of them for keeping on the proper path. With these similarities I find no conflict.

The Apostle Paul on Sexual Identity

It is best not to excite sexual proclivities.

Husbands, Wives and Homosexual Folk, keep the discussions of sex to the closet.

Promotion of Sin is Sin.
Promotion of Homosexual Sex is Sin, is Sin, is Sin.

Do not arouse sexual excitability in one another.

I weep for you, I weep for you. I've been friends with you.
Thou cannot wear that stain upon thy forehead.

A sad decree for some but exalted Peace for many.

Can there be a brotherhood in Christ again?
Can there be "Non Sexual Bro's" clubs of some sort?

Better ideas are discussed, doing thus.

Good Monk

****

Dr. Keown's explanation of the Shaoyang Channels is phenomenal.

I understand better the Jueyin Shaoyang; Shan Han Lun position and connections of exterior and interior.

The team (are there others Dr. Keown would share credit with?) who has made discovery of the Shaoyang association with San Jaio and fascia and Gall bladder (being spotless) with Lymph, deserves to be nominated for the Nobel Prize in Medicine.

The Gall Bladder closed circuit equivalency of a motor, moving bile salts five times through during digestion.

A crucial decision is made through the Gall Bladder of absorbing good fat and extruding bad. Tentacle connections to Yin, artery (shaoyin), endoderm (taiyin), and jueyin (liver).

The Wizard of Oz is an Octopus head and string.

Is that who is making our decisions for us? Tucked snug away in the center of our body. 'neath the liver enfolded.

Another Nobel Prize equivalency is the ideogram of San Jaio.

Continuing kudo's to Dr. Keown's work.

****

The Piezo Electrician - 3rd Installment

The Man who had to refrain from sex, in order to save the world.

Spiritual battles waged in the contemplative man.

Sex is death in the older man. Sex as a human need diminishes.
The struggle comes easier, in denying oneself of sex, so as to preserve oneself.

I believe the third level of human knowledge is the cure for this disease, which physically warps and morally deconstructs.

Those in the third level of human knowledge know that Essence is a Treasured Substance, depleted at ejection. Meditate upon the Pericardium for the antidote.

"La petite mort."

"Sigh"

"La petite mort," says the one who disdains sex, but who is physically apt, with still lingering intervals of well maintained health.

"Sigh," says the healthy good monk.

Jehovah gives this human need.
Jehovah frowns this human need.

"I tell you that anyone who looks at a woman to lust after her has already committed adultery with her in his heart. If your right eye causes you to sin, gouge it out and throw it away. It is better for you to lose one part of your body than for your whole body to be thrown into hell...."

A hard sentence.

The man of knowledge knows.

"Lord, assuage me with greater knowledge upon the sacrifice of this human need I make."

If I could will myself to save the world, could I do so?

There are mistakes of no fault, mistakes, and misfortunes of sex.
There are good fortunes too.

Is masturbation and nocturnal emissions, mistake or mistakes of no fault?
I will not argue any good fortune in masturbation.
Nocturnal emissions are no fault.

Meditate upon the Kidneys!

When images come less in the Mind of the Contemplative Man.
The Devil's work is harder to do.

I have treasured my moments in time of imperfect clarity and clarity reached.
My meditations have me spotless.
I am continuing in good health and peaceful state of mind.

My meditations of the Lou Connecting points have thus me completed, to the depths.
Gall Bladder Octopus Mind upon my Heart.
A Qi worm of connection I felt twixt the two.

My heart problems have been Justified. I feel morally clear and spotless.

****

Why I think Acupuncture is worthy of the Nobel Prize and my formal endorsement of nomination* of Dr .Daniel Keown (and other selected teammates?) to the prize.

Dr. Daniel Keown through his books "The Spark in the Machine" and "The Uncharted Body" delivers a magnificent historical Spectrum of Medicine. In a timeless fractal manner; embryology in modern and technical description unfolds according to the Ancient Structures of Acupuncture and Oriental Medicine. Dr. Keown's work can rightfully be described as a melding of the highest levels of medical knowledge and self understanding.

1. The discovery** of San Jaio as an Organ of Fascia is a Nobel Prize worthy event.

2. Dr. Keown's remarkable job of mapping the unfolding tissues of the Taiyin, Shaoyin, Jueyin, Taiyang, Shaoyang, Yangming channels from embryology to their ultimate anatomical position and physiology confirms applications such as use of the Liver for menstrual disorders and the Pericardium's position of the coronary arteries and treatment thereof. From the ancient traditions of Acupuncture and Oriental Medicine, understanding is expanded of what organs and their physiology are.

3. Dr. Keown weaves together the remarkable correspondences of ancient Chinese Medical ideograms with modern medicine. Exampled by weave and net ideograms predicting thousands of years later the weave net like structures of fascia. Another example is the Gall Bladder's role of being "Spotless" which is an ancient puzzle whose meaning has been elegantly interpreted by Dr. Keown.

Dr. Daniel Keown as both a "Western" and "Eastern" doctor is an ambassador of Medicine across modernity and millennia. "The Spark in the Machine" and "The Uncharted Body" are impressive, masterly done works.

I believe it is time for Acupuncture in Oriental Medicine to win the Nobel Prize upon these and many other grounds.***

Thank you Dr. Keown for inspiring the imagination of those in awareness of Qi.

* I am aware I am unable to nominate anyone for the Nobel Prize.
**I am aware but don't know of others who have also made this connection.
***The author recognizes Nobel Prizes have been awarded for works in Herbal Medicine, but is unaware of any for Acupuncture or Acupuncture Physiology.

****

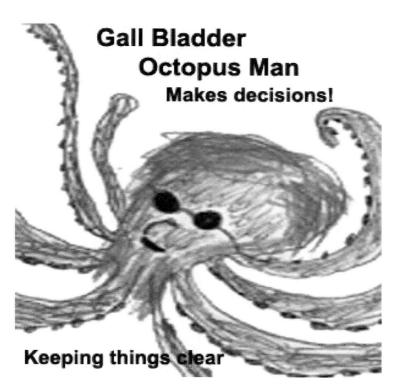

Gall Bladder
Octopus Man
Makes decisions!

Keeping things clear

C'est moi.

Monks live Contemplative Lives. I too have lived a Contemplative Life. I have worked a hundred jobs and taken jobs upon water. I have lived on boats and anchored in many lonely harbors. Inside of all my work was wrapped the greater treasure of leisure. Left to myself in nature, libraries, beautiful places and cities which I sought, or were offered to me. Eating lunches in parks and station yards. The good will of my mother, the traveler and father, the sailor kept me wise and a foot.

Misfortunes of being ill and alone, have been every day Justified in Good Fortune since the day I became aware in meditation, the day I discovered knowledge.

Most of my life has been in leisure, even unto today. Jehovah has generously provided me outdoors where I can much be alone, engaging in secret play.

My perambulations covered 3000 miles back and forth steering a barge and walking mules on the Delaware Canal. I've crossed mountains in the Alps and Alaska. I have napped in meadows, ready to stir at the approach of a bear, or sleeping through its nearby rustle in a bush. I have camped months in water logged tents on beaches, rocky and soft. I have walked a thousand times the shore of Venice to Santa Monica in cloud misted nights. Alone the entire way.

I was born a Contemplative Life. I was born with the Apostles Eye.

Two words H and S.

****

My boat is an Angry Stallion

My boat is problems to be solved.
Desperately

I nearly hang myself with the boom line caught on the back shoulder of my life jacket as I'm drifting backwards towards the dock.

In reverse I turn the boat and get past the luff when facing into the wind. I sail away from the dock, quickly to discover I attached the tiller over the chord latch to the boom line sail connect.

I'll practically have to hold the boom in my hands (again) in the winds of 20-25 knots.

I choose my spot to sail to disembark from the boat to re-rig the rudder. The bay is shallow shortly ahead and it is low tide.

Sailing over the sandy bottom I lift the keel and prepare to loosen sail.
The sail swings 250 degrees in the strong wind. I have to drop the sail

I release the halyard only to discover the line is clove hitched at the top of the mast. The sail isn't dropping and I am being blown in the wind.

Standing on deck I wrestle the sail.
My drift is taking me towards the beach of the kayak rental.

"I will claim distress in a storm," if somebody approaches me.
I manage to drop the sail and paddle to shore.

I am conscious of the obstacle ahead as I re rig the sail and tiller.

I will have to launch the boat into the wind, to the left where a wharf with piers decayed will have to be avoided.

I launch from shore and clear the wharf with five feet. As I go off I am in disbelief of the mistakes I have made and how quickly the problems pile up. It has been my typical experience almost each time out.

Jibbing to in front of our dock, the mast falls upon my head as I drop sail, but I give my wife two thumbs up. She watched everything but is not able to comprehend the multitude of problems that can suddenly befall a sailor.

"In a sailboat prepare to embarrass yourself," said my dad.

That is the attitude I take in front of my neighbors who watch my potential accident filled embarks and returns.

It's an adventure, these problems to be solved, desperately.

"Sailing releases endorphins," says I.

This was my fifth time out, twas a doozy.

From "Dostoevsky, A Writer in His Time" by Joseph Franks.

"For Dostoevsky's morality is similar to what some theologians, speaking of the early Christians, have called "Interim Ethics", that is, an ethics whose uncompromising extremism springs from the lurking imminence of the Day of Judgment and the Final Reckoning; there is no time for anything but the last kiss of reconciliation because, quite literally, there is no "time". page 182

Like Alyosha I belovedly sit at the feet of Father Zossima to listen and observe his teachings. I also like his rival Father Ferapont too. I believe his story is an authentic account. He spotted devils and slammed doors on their tails.   He ate mushrooms and rye bread (when moldy can be psycho tropic).

I believe Father Ferapont was an authentic monk in the Shaoyang Experience.

Dostoevsky was an influence of mine to the Shaoyang Realm when I was young, before I had known.

Dostoevsky probably suffered from cerebral fibrillations during his epileptic attacks. He also faced mock execution in front of a firing squad and four years as a political prisoner in Siberia. His was the Shaoyang Realm experience as well.

Interim ethics; Spiritual exaltation in the imminence of dying.

****

These are the neck stretches I do after having the mast fall on my head. Later in the evening I was getting pain and stiffness, a fair enough warning to stretch. Also a few days prior I compressed my neck by accident, banging my head on our low ceiling when I went to change a light bulb.

This is a stretch from my "Fountain of Youth Stretching" book series.

Last night as I stretched I was tucking my chin to my chest and felt stretches along the cervical spine which provided immediate comfort. This is a type of traction stretch with traction being provided at the shoulder.

If I can save one person from the agonies of neck pain or avoid nerve impingement syndrome with this stretch my job has been done. I have already saved myself. Today my neck feels great with full range of motion and smooth movement.

Instructions on the stretch follow the pictures. The effectiveness of the stretch may be differ depending on the height of the chair you are sitting in and the angle and position of your head tucked to chest.

Consult with your doctor before doing these stretches.

Neck and Shoulder Stretch

Two parts to this stretch

1. Shoulder

Hand is stepped underneath opposite foot.
With traction, lift shoulder (shoulder shrug) upwards against resistance of hand underneath foot. This is an isometric stretch. This stretches the shoulder rotator cuffs.

2. Neck

Reaching behind head, head turns in the direction of the reaching hand. Chin pointed down at chest.

Pull in this direction

3. Perform both these techniques at the same time.

****

I also did this stretch

Shoulder stretch Infraspinatus and Teres Minor (2 of the 4 shoulder rotator cuff muscles) - cross arms at bar, lean back and stretch Shoulder stretch Infraspinatus and Teres Minor (2 of the 4 shoulder rotator cuff muscles) - cross arms at bar, lean back and stretch

These have been excerpted from "Dr. Evan Mahoney Fountain of Youth Stretching" book series available at Amazon.com

The Piezo Electrician will do well to stretch and meditate. These are two complementary components for the fountain of youth.
****

I have written above of my attempts to target the coronary arteries with meditation. Today I read of Pericardium 4 on page 224 Dr. Keown "Uncharted Body," for Myocardial Infarction.

"The heart is the electrical aspect of what we understand as the heart whereas the pericardium is more so the blood and specifically, the coronary vessels."

I meditate on Pericardium 4 (with PC/ Stomach). PC 4 is more proximal (higher up) to the forearm then I am used to. I add Lung 9 and Spleen 10 (influential pt of vessel, invigorate blood). I could feel the funnels of pressure at my wrist. Pressure differentials distal to PC 4, Qi diverged to the heart and Lung. Just like the pictures of Dr. Keown's book, funnels of pressure outlined from my forearm to fingertips.

The dimensions I have undergone in the last 24 hours must be a manifestation of release of Cortisal from my Adrenal Cortex, for the stress involved with the sailing I have been doing. These must be the endorphins I feel after sailing.

These are a strong signal for the body's growth, as it must respond to the new challenges it is environmentally faced with. Last night Qi went into dimensions of ether through my upper body and chest, no blockages, but faint and distant (a concern). I soon slept well and woke up feeling great. Keep stretching, keep growing.

It is a beautiful day after yesterday's storm. The weather forecaster said so.

A school of Jacks (my wife says they look like tuna) have been feeding in circles upon the corner basin where school of minnows are penned in. The Jacks swarm like an Army churning things up in all confusion. Waves of minnows twist in the frenzied current of flashing jaws and tails, hoping for survival. Some have jumped ashore only to be fed on by the egrets.

I trace the movement of the Jacks postprandial as they patrol off the dock. In a school of 200 they swim up and down the nearby channel and track like a mammal in the chop. They surf by me on the waves.

Back at the basin the minnows are alert and nervous, not only for the Jacks but the school of Snook that have come from their place underneath the boat. It appears as if the Snook are herding the minnows like sheep. Is it to protect them, their stock, from the hoarding raids of the Jacks?

Or is it to feed themselves? For some of them do (because I hear their 'snap').

Moments ago inside my kitchen I heard the rumble of the return of the Jacks, devouring the basin. An unendurable length of time, if you are the minnow. They are back again! As I write.

It has been a wonderful glorious day, on Easter too!

Could Jesus be a liar or lunatic? If not (and he is not) then we can only reject (by not believing) or accept him as our Lord.

Notre Dame - To the benevolent help of our lady, we too weep and pray.

The loss of Lord Christ is a mortal loss, shocking the sensibilities.

"Ah, but it so happened Friday, today he has Risen."

This marks our faith and caps our love. He died and has risen for all, for all. Even those who have shocked my sensibilities. The Devil has been defeated. Angels used me and discarded my flesh.

So it feels with an open free heart. I could feel the kink at the Xi cleft point of my heart open up. I am in the latest fractal of Joy, Health, Growth, and Fullness. The cortisol demanded of me a new level. In the greatest efficiency I moved, with stretching and meditation circulating Qi and growing muscle. Otherwise cortisol levels would cause imbalance, turning to fat and depleting essence.

The minnows in far less number were indeed penned in by the pod of Snook who face towards them at a foot away. Throughout the afternoon there were numerous Jack sorties. The Snook didn't fight them off, but sometimes seemed to create distraction or distortion. When a few Jacks did break through to feed, the Snook were snapping with them.

****

Tacking on a Sunfish requires a strong affirmative decision. With force and suddenness you have to push the tiller fully towards the lee, (turning the boat into the wind), lay low on the foredeck to avoid the swing of the boom (and boom line), and shift yourself to the other side of the boat. (To avoid capsize by being caught leeward with the sail).

It is that shifting to the other side the boat which has improved my technique today.

"Do it now," I declared my decision to turn.

More quickly I shifted to the other side of the boat. Out of 6 tacks, I got luffed in the wind once, almost losing my scarf and hat to the water.

Tacking between channel markers and low tide oyster beds, in the moment between back and forward drift, the sail was full but we were still. Then we took off.

****

Thank you Dr. Keown for the wonderful congruency. I congratulate you on your Eight Extraordinary Channels. The subject of which, this two part book series shall both begin and end. I appreciate your pairing of the channels and the respective anatomic and embryological positions they occupy.

Du Mai - Yangqiao
Ren Mai - Yinqiao

Dai Mai - Yang Wei
Chong Mai - Yin Wei

In meditation, accessing these channels uses the same two points bilaterally.

Du Mai - YangQiao
 Small Intestine 3, UB 67 bilaterally.

Ren Mai - YangQiao
 Lung 7, Kidney 6 bilaterally

Dai Mai - Yang Wei
Spleen 5, GB 41 bilaterally

Chong Mai - Yin Wei
PC 6, Spleen 4 bilaterally.

****

I had spasms, convulsions, and electric sparks throughout,
In Myoclonus my body shook.

To activate my Ming Men Fire I meditated on the Spleen / SI with all the 8's. I visualized to my duodenum and Ligament of Trietz connecting my Small Intestine to both the Heart and Spleen. In prolonged durations, deep to my chest, Qi worms slithered down and across my Aorta, like microcosms of all the fibrillations I've ever endured.

I felt a valvular release from the Gall Bladder, central right side. Digestion of potato chips and Kombucha tea has begun in the intestines, my lymphatics are in motor movement.

Resting comfortably on the couch I meditate into dreamlike Archetypes of the Spleen. Jungle rhythms are brought to my attention, coming from Stomach and earth. Sweet happy songs of feasts and celebration, images emerge. Old Hollywood tapped into the Archetypes of Earth (stored in the Spleen). My jungle dreams and Spleen soon shifted.

I had nearly hurt myself and my cat today by absent mindedness when I walk. First, I almost got my leg wedged between boat and car as I tried to squeeze through. Then as I was going to lie on the sofa, I almost knocked the cantilevered table on Plucky.

Seeing the near accident at my feet had me thinking. "Danger, Danger, Danger. I've got to be on guard about accidents."

It is to the Lung / Urinary Bladder I meditated, particularly for the Urinary Bladder's function of guarding and protecting.

I think of Dr. Keowns *Du Mai - Yang Wei* pairing which targets the upper spine and Cerebellum.

With the Lung / UB harmonized combination I also use SI 3, UB 62 bilaterally and target my upper spine and back of head. Qi moves and circulates posterior to my heart where it feels dusty, dry, and deflated. The same thing happens to my right lung. Qi moved to these places where I was seldom aware, where my meditations had yet uncovered. Lobe by Lobe, Qi enfolded the right upper lung. I was encapsulated from within by all light, shining without obstruction in all direction.

Into my right side upper lung, it became as if I had stumbled. I found myself surprisingly in the manger of Christ's birth. It was Mary, the Holy Mother, whose presence was revealed. In this meager but Holy spot she was enrobed, and cradled unseen, her infant son. From all around, God's light did shine protectively, upon this precious scene.

There was my Corporal Soul, closely guarded.

"Aye, it was closely guarded."

By the Lung/ Urinary Bladder and all of the Eight's.

****

Having been touched by the presence of Mary, the Holy Mother
I could not help to grow Angel Wings like Deer Antler upon my back;

Grief is what led me to discover Holy Mother, Mary in my right upper lung. My father needs a … and three …. The doctor was surprised after the … scope that at 87 he exhibits no symptoms. I cried in tears upon the dock, thinking of my father's mortality. I directed my grief energy to the Lung/ Ub to soothe my corporal soul. Soon came thoughts of Love.

"It was my acupuncture." I smiled to myself, which surprised the doctor in regards to my father's condition.

Soon after my dad calls me to tell me he loves me and to also say," it was the acupuncture and ginseng," that surprised the doctor.

My cat is sick, throwing up lots of cold clear phlegm. She sits next to my leg on the bench as we look out over the water. She is tired and sick. I cry to tears for her too, then lay my hand lightly upon her belly. I start with the PC/ Stomach and I jump in Myoclonus. I switch to the Lung /

UB and feel her take a breath underneath my hand. She relaxes, Qi is moving in her too. Using the Lung / UB with The Du - Yangqiao then Ren - Yinqaio channels I think of the Holy Mother Mary, Saintress of grief.

Come now Mary, haven't you heard? It's the resurrection that has occurred.

****

Congratulations again to Dr. Keown. When the timing is right please allow yourself to say, to your wife and children.

"I have been nominated for the Nobel Prize."

It is on sincere terms that we at *The Journal of the Knowledge Pursuant Self* sponsor your election and introduction to the Nobel Prize Award Committee given for Medicine, of whom sadly we have no contacts.

As a journal for serious consideration, we offer our own prize worthy discoveries. Though the Interpretation of Dreams may sound to you, cheap, is it not simple logic to dream upon the three levels of human needs and identify which of those human needs was represented? Surely, you can accept the pairing of these expressed needs in dreams to the appropriate organ?

This my friends, is my true election; Organ Centered Consciousness, and everything meaningful behind that phrase. From revisiting of social luminaries Freud and Jung (and lesser known Sarno), we have developed our PTSD therapy of Kidney / San Jaio. "Fear is a physical disease and it resides in the Kidney's" With Saam Medical Meditation we access deeply into the conscious and unconscious phenomena.

We meditators in Qi have to leave it here, we don't want to overwhelm you with our brilliance. We do question dear reader of your own experience in Saam Medical Meditation? Please let us know.

"Au Revoir", this has been an exceedingly fun and exciting journal.

Saam Meditation/ Acupuncture

Five (e) – Book Series by Dr. Evan Mahoney

Available at Amazon.com

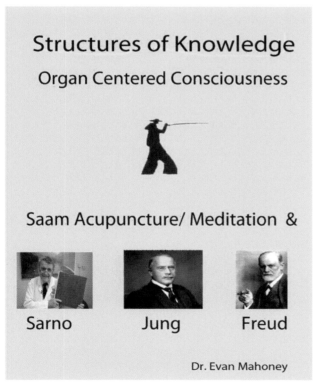

Printed in Great Britain
by Amazon